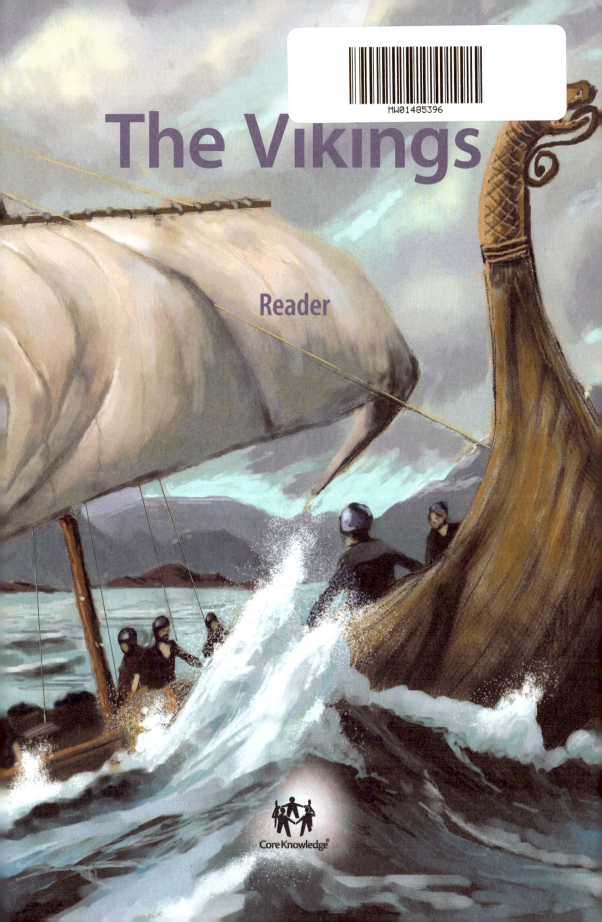

The Vikings

Reader

Core Knowledge®

ISBN: 978-1-68380-100-9

The Vikings

Table of Contents

The Vikings
Reader
Core Knowledge History and Geography™

Chapter 1
The Vikings

Mighty Warriors A thousand years ago, a seafaring people called Vikings lived in northwest Europe. They made their homes in the region now known as Scandinavia. Vikings were skilled shipbuilders and sailors. Their ships, called longships, were so sleek they seemed to fly through water.

The Vikings were also fierce warriors. Sometimes they would **raid** towns and take property by force. In the story that follows, you will learn more about the Vikings.

Long ago a young Viking boy named Ivar walked down a grassy path along a deep, narrow inlet of the sea, called a **fjord** (/fee*ord/). The grass was still wet with dew.

Vocabulary

raid, v. to attack suddenly and with force

fjord, n. a deep and narrow portion of the sea that stretches inland, with high cliffs on either side

The morning sun was still low in the sky. But Ivar had been at work since before sunrise. Ivar's family lived on a farm. He had to get up very early each day to milk the goats and cows, and care for the other animals, too.

Viking children were expected to help support the family by doing chores.

Viking children did not go to school. Most people farmed, and boys and girls were expected to help with the chores. As children grew, they learned more skills. For example, boys were taught to fight with weapons, and girls learned to spin wool and make clothes. This training prepared young people for their roles in adulthood.

Ivar was also learning to be a **blacksmith**. As soon as he was done with his chores, he had to run to the village blacksmith's shop to help make some iron tools.

When Ivar had any free time, he spent it with other boys, learning how to hunt and fish and ride horses. Music and board games were also popular among both boys and girls. Viking childhood did not last long, though! Young people had to take on adult roles as soon as they could.

In addition to his work at home, Ivar was learning how to be a blacksmith.

A Viking boy might look forward to one day getting his own sword.

Today the blacksmith was pleased that Ivar had kept his promise to stop daydreaming when they had work to do. Yesterday, Ivar's mind had wandered. He had accidentally knocked over a large water bucket. As a result, the blacksmith had become very angry—and very wet.

Ivar hoped that the blacksmith would make a sword for him, but he did not ask about it today. Ivar thought he would wait a few days. He wanted to give the blacksmith a chance to forget about what had happened with the water bucket.

Viking Raiders

As he worked, Ivar thought about his father, Tor. Ivar's father was a Viking **jarl** (/yahr*ul/), or chief. He had been away from home for many months, leading a long voyage at sea.

> **Vocabulary**
>
> **jarl,** n. a Viking chief

A Viking raid was a terrifying event.

Tor the Jarl and his men had taken a voyage to **plunder** towns, villages, and churches near seacoasts and along rivers. The Vikings raided these places with their swift longships. They stole treasure, burned buildings, and took captives. The Vikings demanded that the families or friends of the captives pay a **ransom**. If they refused, the Vikings forced the captured people into slavery. The Vikings killed anyone who tried to stop them. Everyone feared the Viking raiders.

The Vikings had a special saying for going on this kind of raiding voyage. They said Tor and his men had gone "a-viking."

The Viking Alphabet

Ivar was happy because he had just finished carving a special **rune** stone as a

Vocabulary

plunder, v. to take something by force

ransom, n. money paid to release someone being held captive

rune, n. a letter of the Viking alphabet

Viking Runes

ᚠ	ᚢ	ᚦ	ᚬ	ᚱ	ᚴ	ᚼ	ᚾ	ᛁ	ᛅ	ᛋ	ᛏ	ᛒ	ᛘ	ᛚ	ᛦ
f	u o v	th	a	r	k g	h	n	i e y	a	s	t d	b p	m	l	z/R

The top of this chart shows the sixteen Viking runes of the Futhark (/footh*ark). Under each rune are the sounds the rune relates to in English.

present for his father. Runes were the letters of the Viking alphabet known as the Futhark (/footh*ark). Before Tor left to go a-viking, he had told Ivar to learn rune carving. Ivar obeyed his father. He had practiced every day. He was now very good at carving the shapes of the Futhark. This alphabet had sixteen letters, or runes. Ivar hoped his father would be pleased.

The Vikings used runes to record information about important events and preserve the memory of important people. Runes were rarely used to record stories, or narratives. The Vikings also believed that runes had magical powers.

The Futhark

Each rune had a sound that relates to letters in the English alphabet we use today. (The first six letters or sounds spell out the word *Futhark*.) Some runes were used for more than one sound. For example, the rune ↑ had the same sound as the English letters "t" and "d." One rune was used for a sound we do not have in English—the sound "zir" or "z/R."

Chapter 2
Traders and Raiders

Coming Home Ivar was startled by the blast of a loud horn. The sound signaled the approach of a Viking ship. Ivar looked down the fjord. He saw that his father's great longship, with its crew of **oarsmen**, was about to come ashore near the village.

The Big Question

How did the Vikings get the riches they brought back to their homeland?

Vocabulary

oarsmen, n. on a ship, those who are responsible for rowing

Viking longships were not enclosed. They had large square sails. The longships often traveled in groups and could withstand very stormy weather.

Ivar's father and his crew had been a-viking for more than a year. The horn sounded again. The sailors cheered as the ship approached the shore.

Four men wearing animal hides jumped from the ship onto the beach, shouting for the others to follow. These warriors were called **berserkers**. This word comes from the Viking words for "bear shirt." Berserkers believed they could not be wounded. So, they fought without armor for protection,

wearing only bearskin shirts. As they charged their victims, they let out terrifying screams. With their screams and their clothes, the berserkers appeared like wild animals. Of all the Vikings, they were the most fearless—and the most frightening.

The next man into the water was Ivar's father, Tor the Jarl. He ordered the men to lower the sail, raise their oars from the water, and **tow** the great ship onto the beach.

Ivar ran fast down the pathway that led across the steep wall of the fjord to the beach. He hoped to surprise his father. Ivar had grown while his father was gone. He wondered if his father would notice. "I'll bet Father won't believe how big I've become," Ivar thought. Suddenly his foot slipped and he almost fell down the rocky path. Fortunately, he was able to catch himself and break his fall. He sighed with relief and then started down the path again, more slowly this time.

Father and Son

On the beach, the Vikings were too busy towing the ship to notice Ivar. He could still surprise his father. Ivar felt a rock give way under his foot. It made a loud crash as it bounced down the path, followed by several more crashes as it rolled down to the beach.

Tor noticed the tumbling rock and turned around. He spotted Ivar before his son had run very far down the path.

"Ivar!" Tor called. Clearly, his father still recognized him. "Go back to the village. Fetch wagons and help carry this treasure to our house. And bring Olaf the shipbuilder back to make repairs to the ship. And, boy, tell your mother to prepare a feast!"

A Viking feast meant lots of food—and lots of fun!

"Yes, Father! Welcome home, Father!" Ivar shouted as he turned to run back up the path.

"I see that you have grown taller," Tor called after his son. "Perhaps we will see how well you fare wrestling your father tonight."

"Oh, no, Father! Not even the berserkers will wrestle Tor the Jarl!" Ivar laughed.

Mixed Cargo

The crew unloaded the **cargo** from the great ship. There were bags of silver coins, silver candlesticks and **goblets**, jewelry, glass, silk fabric, and barrels of wine.

Some of the cargo came from trading with people in far-off lands. But most of it had been stolen when the Viking warriors attacked other people's ships or towns along the coasts and rivers of Europe.

> **Vocabulary**
>
> **cargo,** n. goods transported by a ship, plane, or truck
>
> **goblet,** n. a large container used for drinking

On Tor's ship, there was also human cargo—prisoners captured by the Vikings during their raids. The berserkers threw these people off the ship into the shallow water. They were captives who belonged to the jarl. They would spend the rest of their lives in slavery unless they were freed in return for payment of a ransom.

Vikings traded throughout Europe and raided unsuspecting victims.

Chapter 3
Viking Sailors and Ships

Ships for Trading and Raiding

The jarl's family lived on a farm nestled between the fjords and the mountains. Ivar ran past the farm's stables and workshops, shouting for his brothers. He found them playing outside the family's house.

The Big Question

Why were ships so important to the Viking way of life?

"Father is home! His ship just arrived in the big fjord!" The boys stopped playing and stared at their older brother.

"Don't just stand there, you two! Harald, find Mother, and tell her the good news. Rolf, go with Harald, and let Mother know that Father needs all the wagons and lots of people to unload his cargo."

Ivar's brothers were playing when he came home with the news of their father's return.

Ivar kept running. Soon he reached the sheltered beach. There he found Olaf the Shipbuilder hard at work.

Olaf and his fellow Vikings built some of the best ships in the world. They lived in Scandinavia, a place with island, fjords, mountains and forests and very few roads. So, they usually traveled by water. They had to have excellent ships.

Olaf and his crew were just finishing a large cargo ship. Ivar was always amazed at how much a cargo ship could hold. These great vessels could carry all the things the Vikings needed when they moved to faraway places. This happened a lot. Their homeland was crowded, and there was not enough good land to farm. It saddened Ivar to think that many Viking families had to move.

As towns in the Viking homeland grew and became crowded, many Viking families had to move.

A Young Boy's Dream

Ivar did not want to leave his homeland, but he longed to sail on one of these great ships. He had listened to the stories of the old sailors. He already knew how to find his way by using the sun and the stars as guides. And he knew what to do if his ship ever got lost at sea: The Vikings had noticed that birds at sea usually flew toward land. So, they took caged birds with them on their ocean voyages. If they became lost, the sailors simply released the birds—and followed them to safety.

Ivar imagined what it would be like to sail on a long journey. He knew that at the beginning of the voyage, the ship sailed close to the coastline and beached on land for the evening. The sailors would light campfires and hang big cooking pots over them.

Viking ships were sleek and fast, but while at sea they offered little protection to the people on board.

When the ship sailed into the open ocean, the voyage would become more difficult. The sea might be dotted with icebergs. The waves could be fierce. While at sea, there were no cabins on Viking ships to protect the sailors from bad weather. The sailors would be cold and wet most of the time. But when the ship was **moored**, or at anchor, a tent-like awning could be used to provide shelter.

Building a Viking Ship

Olaf's crew also built Viking warships. Ivar saw one of these mighty vessels resting at anchor nearby. Olaf had carved a serpent-like creature on the warship's curved **prow** to frighten enemies. Ivar imagined the ship's brightly colored sail full in the wind.

Right now, Olaf the Shipbuilder was carving a tree trunk into the long **mast** that would support the cargo ship's sail. All around him, workers were chopping and pounding the oak boards of the great ship.

Olaf shouted, "Ivar, what brings you here today?"

"My father has returned," Ivar shouted back. "His longship needs repairs."

"What a lucky time for the jarl to come home!" shouted Olaf. "His old shipmate, Sigurd the Storyteller, is visiting me now. He has just returned from Greenland. We will bring Sigurd with us. It will be a nice surprise for Tor."

The storyteller was an important person to the Vikings. Not only did he tell stories and recite poems, he also brought news from faraway places.

Vocabulary

moored, adj. secured in place using chains, ropes, or an anchor

prow, n. the pointed front end of a ship

mast, n. a large vertical post on a ship that helps hold up the sails

Serpent-like or dragon-like creatures were carved on a ship's curved prow.

Chapter 4
Eric the Red

A Viking Explorer That evening, everyone gathered together around a roaring fire for an evening of storytelling. Ivar's mother and some other village women had also prepared a wonderful feast.

The Big Question

Why did Eric the Red name the land west of Iceland, Greenland?

Vikings gathered around the fire for an evening of storytelling.

Long tables had been laid out. They were piled with roasted deer and wild boar, dried whale meat, flat breads and cheese, and berries and apples.

After the **feast,** Ivar waited patiently for the storytelling to begin. As a **hush** fell over the group, Tor the Jarl announced, "We welcome Sigurd the Storyteller."

Ivar and every other child scampered to sit at the feet of the storyteller. Sigurd then spoke in a clear, strong voice.

The News from Greenland

"Tor, the news I bring from Greenland began long ago, when you and I were boys. These young people sitting here do not know the beginning of the story as we do. So for them, I will tell the story of Eric the Red.

"We all know of the land to the west of us called Iceland. Many Viking families have moved there. Some of us have sailed to trade with those who live there. Life in Iceland is hard because there is not enough good farmland. Many families there must hunt and fish to stay alive. Eric the Red was born to such a family.

"When he was a boy, Eric learned to hunt seal and walrus on the frozen seas north of Iceland. Eric was very brave, but he had a bad temper.

Sigurd the Storyteller entertained people with news about Vikings in different parts of the world.

"When he was a young man, Eric killed two men. Because he had broken the law, Eric lost his home and was **banished** from Iceland for three years. For a Viking, this was a harsh punishment.

"Eric needed a place to live for those three years. He had heard stories of a new land to the west of Iceland. So he and some companions sailed off in search of it.

"When Eric found the new land, it was surrounded by ice. He could not explore the area during the winter because the sea around it was frozen. He did not find a good place to live until the summer, when he could explore by ship.

Eric the Red hoped to bring Vikings back to settle in Greenland.

"Although the storms were worse than those in Iceland, and most of the land was covered with ice, Eric decided to stay. He found some reasonably good farmland. He also hoped others would sail from Iceland to join him. So, when three years had passed, Eric traveled back to Iceland. He imagined the people there would want to move to a green place. So he told them that the land he had found was called Greenland.

New Settlers

"Eric returned to Greenland. Traveling with him were twenty-five ships full of eager adventurers. They left Iceland on a gentle summer wind. But soon terrible storms forced many of the ships to turn back. In the end, four hundred people reached Greenland in fourteen ships. They settled there with Eric the Red as their leader.

"They soon discovered that there wasn't that much good farmland in Greenland. And there were no forests for timber. But there were fish, seals, walruses, and whales off the coast, so the settlers hunted and fished. They traded sealskins, walrus tusks, and whale bones with other Vikings for what they could not grow or make.

"Now that I have told you of Eric the Red," Sigurd said, "I will tell you what we have learned from Greenland recently."

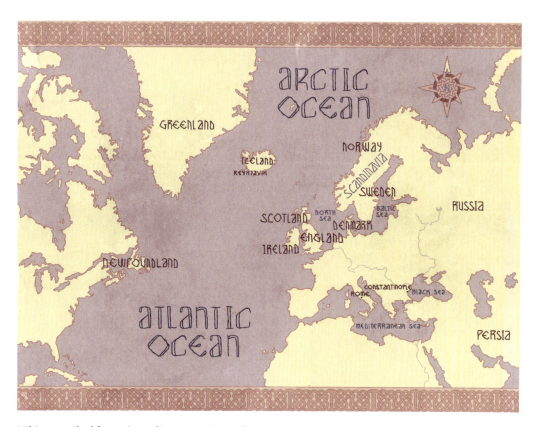

Vikings sailed from Scandinavia to Greenland.

Chapter 5
Leif Eriksson

From Greenland to Vineland

"I promised to tell you what we have heard from faraway Greenland." Sigurd the Storyteller smiled as he looked upon the crowd. Every face had turned his way. Ivar was sitting at Sigurd's feet.

The Big Question

Why might Vikings have once believed that Greenland was the end of the world?

Ivar had never seen Vikings act this way at a feast. Usually, there was lots of laughter, dancing, and loud merrymaking. But when Sigurd the Storyteller spoke, his listeners sat in respectful silence.

Ivar wondered if he could ever be a storyteller like Sigurd. The storyteller had traveled to many lands and had known many great Viking heroes. He knew the stories of the gods and taught them to the Viking children.

VALKYRIES

HOD

BALDER

GGA

TYR

THRYM

SIF

FREYJA

THOR

LOKI

SIGYN

Vikings believed their gods lived in Asgard (/as*gahrd/). Within Asgard there were twelve kingdoms, and each important god had a home in one of them. Vikings told stories about their gods and giants, including the giant Thrym. You can see Thrym in the illustration.

Sigurd also knew all the great Viking poems. "How could anyone have so much knowledge?" Ivar marveled. Ivar promised himself he would ask Sigurd to teach him to be a storyteller. He pictured himself standing in front of his father and the other Vikings, sharing the news from faraway places while they quietly listened with great respect.

Ivar's daydream was interrupted by an uncomfortable feeling. He realized that Sigurd was staring right at him. The great storyteller was talking to him!

"Ivar knows Greenland is at the end of the world. Stand up, Ivar. Tell me, is that true?"

"Yes, sir!" Ivar was glad he knew the answer. "Everyone knows that!"

Sigurd smiled again. "Everyone, Ivar, except those who have heard of the most recent events. For we now know that there are great lands to the west of Greenland that some Vikings have explored.

"Bjarni Herjolfson (/byahr*ni/her*yolf*son/), another great sailor, was the first Viking to see this new land. It happened when a great storm carried his longship far past Greenland. When the storm passed, Bjarni saw land in the distance. But he was eager to reach home, so he sailed back to Greenland," Sigurd told the crowd.

"When Bjarni arrived in Greenland, he told the story of what he had seen to Eric the Red and to Eric's son, Leif Eriksson. The two Vikings were eager to explore this new land.

"Leif Eriksson then bought Bjarni's longship. Leif asked his friends, who were also eager to go exploring, to be his crew. Like his father, Leif was strong and brave and loved adventure. But Leif did

The Vikings were great explorers. From Scandinavia they sailed as far east as Russia and as far west as North America.

not have his father's hot temper. He was a calm and thoughtful young man. Although Eric the Red did not go with them, the explorers sailed to the land Bjarni had seen. They later called this land Vineland, or 'Wineland.' They chose this name because wild grapes grew there. Vineland had rich **pastures** and forests and plenty of animals to hunt. Leif and his crew stayed in Vineland for the winter. When spring came, they sailed back to Greenland.

Vocabulary

pasture, n. land covered with grass on which farm animals feed

Today, we know that what the Vikings called Vineland is Newfoundland in North America.

"On the way back to Greenland, Leif and his crew rescued Vikings who had been shipwrecked. In return, Leif was given the ship's cargo. Ever since then, Leif has been called 'Leif the Lucky.'"

Sigurd put his arm around Ivar's shoulders and said, "As my longship was leaving Greenland, we saw cargo ships loading farm tools and animals. Vikings sailing those ships will soon settle in Vineland.

"So now you know Ivar, Greenland is not at the end of the world."

Tor the Jarl rose to speak. He held a carved rune stone high over his head.

"Tonight is a time of great honor. Sigurd honors us with his important news. Ivar, who worked hard at carving, honors his father with this rune stone."

Cargo ships carried farm animals and tools to Vineland, to help support Viking settlements there.

Chapter 6
Viking Gods and Myths

Religion of the Vikings The Vikings, who were also called the **Norse**, told stories called **myths**. These stories were meant to explain things about their world that they could not understand.

The Big Question

How did myths help the Vikings make sense of their world?

Vocabulary

Norse, n. people who lived in Scandinavia long ago

myth, n. an idea or story that many people believe but is not true

Norse myths are not unlike the myths of ancient Greece or other ancient peoples. They tell about many powerful gods and goddesses. The Vikings believed that the gods were enemies of the evil giants. The chief god Odin killed the evil frost giant with help from his brothers. Then Odin and his brothers made the world from the dead giant's huge body. They made the ocean from his blood. They made the mountains from his bones and the trees from his hair. And they made the sky from the top of his head.

Vikings believed that a tree called Yggdrasill (/ihg*druh*sihl/) held up the world. Here you see Odin's eight-legged horse, Sleipner (/*slep*neer/).

The Vikings believed that a tree called Yggdrasill (/ihg*druh*sihl/), or the world tree, held up the universe. The top of the tree stretched into the heavens. Its three roots reached down to the **underworld**, to the land of the giants, and to Asgard, the land of the gods. A great serpent, or snake, always chewed at the tree's roots. The serpent tried to make the tree fall and bring the world down with it.

Home of the Gods

Asgard was the home of the gods. It had twelve **realms**, one for each of the twelve important gods. Odin was the ruler. He always wanted to know everything. Each morning Odin sent out his two ravens, Thought and Memory, to fly around the world. The birds brought back news to him. Odin loved knowledge so much that he gave up one of his eyes for a drink from the Well of **Wisdom**.

Odin lived in a palace called Valhalla. When a Viking died in battle, one of Odin's beautiful **maidens**, called the Valkyries (/val*keer*eez/), picked up the dead warrior from the battlefield. Then she carried him on her swift warhorse to Valhalla. These warriors lived forever in Valhalla, fighting and telling stories. The Vikings believed that to live in Valhalla was the greatest honor a warrior could achieve.

The strongest of the gods was Odin's son, Thor. He had a quick temper but a kindly heart. Thor was the god of thunder.

Odin, father of the Norse gods, lived in a palace called Valhalla.

He rode a wagon pulled by two goats when he traveled. Thor struck his great hammer to make thunder and rain for the crops. He also fought against evil giants and protected the Norse people.

The Norse god Thor rode a wagon pulled by two goats.

How Thor Got His Hammer

All the goddesses in Asgard were lovely, but none had hair as beautiful as Thor's wife, Sif. She watched over the growing of grain, which ripened to the same color as her golden hair.

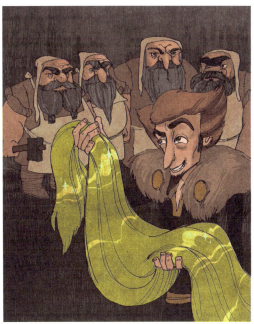

Loki had dwarves make new hair for Sif out of gold.

One night, while Sif slept, Loki, the trickster, crept into her bedroom and cut off all her beautiful hair. Sif woke up and discovered that her hair was gone. She screamed and then collapsed with grief. Thor was furious. He searched everywhere for Loki. He knew that this was the work of the trickster. When Thor finally found Loki, he threatened to break every bone in his body. But Loki promised he would make up for his mean trick. He would go to the land of dwarves and have them make new hair out of gold for Sif.

Loki got the dwarves to make not only Sif's golden hair, but also a magic hammer for Thor. Thor could strike the hammer as hard as possible but it would never be damaged. Also, when Thor threw the hammer, he would always hit his target. In addition, the hammer would always return to his hand. These were just some

Thor's hammer had many special powers.

of the hammer's special powers. Thor could even make it small enough to carry inside his shirt.

At first the gods thought Loki was funny. But then his tricks became too mean. Loki eventually caused so much trouble in Asgard that the gods tied him up and locked him in a dark cave. Loki had to remain there until the end of the world, which would happen as a battle between the gods and the giants.

How the Days of the Week Got Their Names

Did you know that you use words from Norse myths almost every day? That is because four days of the week—Tuesday, Wednesday,

Thursday, and Friday—are named after Norse gods that the Vikings worshiped.

Tuesday is named for Tyr (/tihr/), the Viking god of war and justice. He was also known as the one-handed god, who lost his hand to a wolf named Fenrir.

Wednesday is named for Woden (/who*dun/). *Woden* is the English name for Odin, the Vikings' chief god. Odin could predict the future. He could also change his shape to travel unnoticed.

Which god do you think Thursday is named for? "Thor's day" honors the Norse god of thunder and lightning.

Friday is named for Frigg, the wife of Odin and mother of Balder, the god of goodness. Her name in German is *Friia*.

God	Day of the Week
Tyr	Tuesday
Woden (Odin)	Wednesday
Thor	Thursday
Frigg (Friia)	Friday

Glossary

B

banish, v. to force someone to leave and stay away from a place (22)

berserker, n. one of the most fearless and frightening Viking warriors (10)

blacksmith, n. a type of craftsperson who makes iron tools by hand (4)

C

cargo, n. goods transported by a ship, plane, or truck (12)

F

feast, n. a large meal held to celebrate a day or event (22)

fjord, n. a deep and narrow portion of the sea that stretches inland, with high cliffs on either side (2)

G

goblet, n. a large container used for drinking (12)

H

hush, n. silence (22)

J

jarl, n. a Viking chief (5)

M

maiden, n. a young, unmarried woman (34)

mast, n. a large vertical post on a ship that helps hold up the sails (18)

moored, adj. secured in place using chains, ropes, or an anchor (18)

myth, n. an idea or story that many people believe but is not true (32)

N

Norse, n. people who lived in Scandinavia long ago (32)

O

oarsmen, n. on a ship, those who are responsible for rowing (8)

P

pasture, n. land covered with grass on which farm animals feed (29)

plunder, v. to take something by force (6)

prow, n. the pointed front end of a ship (18)

R

raid, v. to attack suddenly and with force (2)

ransom, n. money paid to release someone being held captive (6)

realm, n. a kingdom (34)

rune, n. a letter of the Viking alphabet (6)

T

tow, v. to drag (10)

U

underworld, n. a place where it was believed that people went when they died (34)

W

wisdom, n. extensive knowledge or experience (34)

CKHG™

Core Knowledge HISTORY AND GEOGRAPHY™

Subject Matter Expert

Angus Somerville M.Litt., Associate Professor, English Language and Literature, Brock University

Illustration and Photo Credits

Brittany Tingey: Cover C, 26–27, 33, 35, 36, 37, 37a, 38

Daniel Hughes: 6, 13

Jacob Wyatt: Cover A, 24, 25, 30

Scott Hammond: Cover D, i, iii, 1, 8–9, 31

Steve Morrison: Cover B, 2–3, 4, 5, 11, 14–15, 16, 17, 19, 20–21, 23, 29